The Illustrated AWS Cloud

A Guide to Help You on Your Cloud Practitioner Journey

Jen Looper

Denise Yu

WILEY

ABOUT THE AUTHORS

Jen Looper is the Head of Academic Advocacy at AWS with more than 23 years of experience as a web and mobile developer specializing in creating cross-platform mobile and web apps. A published author, Jen has written *Computer Science for Kids* (`https://cs4kids.club`), a textbook aligned to CSTA standards for grades 6–8 published by Wiley. She's a multilingual multiculturalist with a passion for web technologies, applied machine learning, and discovering new things every day. With a PhD in medieval French literature, Jen's area of focus is curriculum development and the application of sound pedagogy to technical topics. Visit Jen's personal site at `www.jenlooper.com`.

Denise Yu is a software engineering manager and occasional illustrator. She has spoken at conferences around the world on topics ranging from distributed computing to competitive debating. She holds an MSc in Social Policy from the London School of Economics and a BA in Economics from Columbia University. You can learn more about Denise at `https://deniseyu.io`.

ABOUT THE TECHNICAL EDITOR

As a Principal Developer Advocate with AWS, **Seth Eliot** helps builders architect and implement resilient, scalable systems in the Cloud. Previously, he was Reliability Lead for AWS Well-Architected. Before that, as Principal Solutions Architect, he worked hands-on with Amazon engineers to optimize how they use AWS for the services that power the massive-scale systems behind `Amazon.com`. You can follow Seth on Twitter `@setheliot`, or on LinkedIn at `www.linkedin.com/in/setheliot`.

ACKNOWLEDGMENTS

Thanks to Seth Eliot, my colleague at Amazon, for his rigorous technical editing of this work, as well as for the critiques by AWS Community Builders, including Marty Henderson and Wayne Scarano. I'd especially like to thank my family for their continual support of my projects.

—Jen

CONTENTS

Chapter 5: Being Frugal with Billing and Pricing   156

INTRODUCTION

You might have heard of Cloud computing and have wondered how it pertains to you. You may be familiar with how you **consume** Cloud services, which happens every time you commit code to a remote repository, order a pizza via a mobile app, or review a book you bought on Amazon, but you'd like to go deeper and learn how to **build** in the Cloud. It's an exciting field in which to specialize, and one way you can do so is by diving into the basics that will help you get started working in the Cloud. This book focuses on the Amazon Web Services (AWS) Cloud, comprised of more than 200 services delivered from a global network of data centers into your own home and office seamlessly, securely, and in a cost-effective, scalable manner.

   This book guides your knowledge of how you can become a Cloud practitioner in the AWS Cloud, focusing first on basics that pertain to Cloud computing in general and then diving deeper into the most typical services you'll encounter in the AWS Cloud as you boost your knowledge of Cloud computing. By the end of the book, you will be well on your way to passing the AWS Cloud Practitioner Exam, a foundational exam that helps you embark on your career in Cloud computing. The book assumes no knowledge of Cloud computing, just a curiosity about what you can do in the Cloud and how AWS can help you achieve your goals.

TIP: For more information and a deeper dive into concepts and AWS services, visit `https://aws.amazon.com` and read through the product pages and documentation. We've also built a handy website at `http://illustratedaws.cloud`, where there are lists of learning platforms to try and links to visit to deepen your knowledge.

You might notice that some of the service names vary in the text. A service such as the serverless compute service formally entitled AWS Lambda might be discussed as simply Lambda. This is for brevity and simplicity. In addition, AWS services are often described via acronyms, but every beginner finds those confusing, so we introduce each service via its formal name with the acronym in parentheses. For example, Amazon Elastic Compute Cloud (Amazon EC2) is best remembered as simply EC2. If you get confused, use the search tool at the AWS website to look up the acronyms. A useful tool for quick lookups of computing terminology is `https://aws.amazon.com/what-is`.

In this book, you'll follow four friends—Spike, a senior software reliability engineer; Laurel, a patient project manager; Jeffie, an enthusiastic junior developer; and Bev, a skilled systems architect—as they learn alongside you how the Cloud can help them do their work more easily, efficiently, and painlessly.

Spike

Laurel

Jeffie

Bev

The black-and-white cartoons in the book are designed to give you visual cues to help you remember the concepts you're learning in the text. Go ahead and color in the images if that helps make your learning more relaxing and enjoyable and helps you better remember the concepts. Are you ready to join your new friends on a journey into the Cloud? Let's go!

CHAPTER ONE

Getting Started with Cloud Concepts

Welcome to Chapter 1. In this chapter, you learn what Cloud computing can offer your business. Specifically, this chapter covers the following topics:

- Benefits of Cloud computing
- AWS Cloud economics
- The total cost of ownership
- Reducing costs by moving to the Cloud
- Cloud architecture design principles
- The Well-Architected Framework

By the end of this chapter, you will be able to define the Cloud and describe its many uses. Let's get started!

What Is Cloud Computing?

Imagine you're planning a wonderful camping trip with your friends. You're into the concept of "roughing it," but you have your limits! Do you really need to sew your own sleeping bags, craft your own tents, drag some rocks around to make a fire pit, and rub two sticks together to make a campfire? Probably not! Instead, you might take a trip to your local camping supply store and buy a pup tent kit, a mess kit, and one of those cool camp cook stoves with a little butane fuel container. Once you're geared up, you can free your attention to enjoying the great outdoors in the company of your friends!

Cloud computing is a little like that visit to the store to source your gear, rather than building it all yourself. Instead of managing your own servers in your own office, you can use **the Cloud**, which is a set of services available to you to conduct your business's needs over the Internet. You can store files in the Cloud, manage data in various regions, connect your systems together, and do much more by using Cloud computing. You probably use it every day without even realizing it.

Whenever you open a mobile app to reserve a spot at your local campground, you are using the Cloud to make the connection between the device you hold in your hand, the Internet, and the campground's system for taking your reservation. This is the difference between the client (your phone and its browser or app) and the server (the machine that exists somewhere else and handles your requests).

The Cloud—the machine or "server" that exists in a data center somewhere not too far from you—takes care of the transactions needed to make your camping outing perfect, including gathering your personal information, storing it safely and privately, notifying the campground to reserve a designated spot, and transferring your payment from your bank account to theirs. It's such a seamless experience that people hardly think about it nowadays, but the technology behind it is worth a deep dive.

Cloud computing brings with it a lot of benefits that can help any business or individual succeed in achieving their goals. It has six specific benefits that are worth understanding well. Diving deep into these topics will guide you as you start your journey to becoming a Cloud practitioner. So let's go!

Global Reach

If you are managing your own servers, including the hardware, software, and networking capabilities that you need to keep your business systems running, imagine how complex your task becomes when you need to reach customers in the far corners of the Earth. Cloud computing offers the ability to "go global" as quickly as you like.

The idea of going global isn't so much that your systems, now ported to the cloud, aren't already accessible in many different parts of the Internet-connected world. The benefit to Cloud computing on AWS is that you can do it *well*. By deploying your business systems globally, their *latency* is reduced.

NOTE: *Latency* is the amount of time needed for information to travel across a network. If an application is deployed closer to the user, it takes less time to arrive.

Going global allows folks to deliver a fast experience to their customers worldwide.

Economies of Scale

When you think of yourself and your capabilities, you're only able to achieve a limited number of things each day. That's normal! You need to eat, rest, and practice some self-care during your busy day. There's an expression, however, that "many hands make light work." Within the context of Cloud computing, the same analogy applies.

A huge company such as Amazon can serve thousands upon thousands of customers, and because they have this scale, they can spread costs across many customers and reduce pricing for their services. In this way, we talk about how the AWS Cloud benefits its customers due to its massive economies of scale. More customers means more services delivered at better prices because their usage is combined in the Cloud and prices can be better managed at scale. It's a bit like asking your friend group to pool their money to pay for a campsite rental for a weekend camping trip.

Agility

Everyone loves convenience. The connected world in which many people are fortunate to live allows a car to be summoned at the press of a button, rather than having to rent one every time you visit a new city or own a car if you don't use it all the time. In Cloud computing, similar agility is displayed when a developer can quickly spin up a database and provision it for use by a company in just a few clicks.

We are so used to doing this nowadays that it seems trivial, but imagine the days before Cloud computing made it easy. You can make decisions much more quickly now that so many resources are a click away on an Internet-enabled device connected to the Cloud. Your ability to conduct experiments and change your mind is enhanced as well. Within a Cloud computing context, you are able to "try before you buy," sampling the ability of a various Cloud-connected service before deciding if it's right for you, turning it off if it doesn't meet your needs, or ramping up your usage if it proves just right.

Elasticity, Scalability, and Availability

When you are trying to make plans to build something for use by different types of customers worldwide, it can be daunting to try to make plans about how much compute you need, how much storage you need, what services you have to leverage and how they should all connect. Cloud computing solves this problem in a really neat way.

NOTE: In the context of the Cloud, **compute** refers to the processing power, memory, networking capability, and storage used for software computation.

AWS offers a suite of highly available online services that powers workloads, providing secure, *elastic* (resizable) compute capacity in the Cloud. You learn more about these services in Chapter 4.

Instead of asking you to plan up front how much computing power your applications need, you can set up your Cloud computing infrastructure mirroring your current needs and then quickly add more capacity as the demand for your services expands or contracts. With Cloud computing, this is possible. You can quickly scale your infrastructure's size and scope up and down, depending on the resources needed or not needed at a given time.

Cloud computing offers the promise of high availability, meaning your sites will be up and running with minimal downtime with a very high percentage of time that your workloads in the Cloud are available to be used.

NOTE: In Cloud computing, a **workload** is defined as "a set of components that together bring business value." Websites and dashboards reflecting the output of databases are examples of workloads.

Availability is the amount of time your workloads are available to be used, divided by a given period, such as a month or a year. So, if your website, for example, is down for five minutes every year for scheduled or unscheduled reasons, its availability is described as 99.999 percent. This would be described as highly available, with "five nines" of availability, and would be a promise you could make to your customers about your reliability. Since you pay more for business systems that require very high uptime, you need to decide how much downtime you can tolerate in order to budget correctly.

How does AWS make sure that services can be available? In general, it helps enable three elements.

- That there are no single points of failure
- That systems are redundant and fail over at reliable crossover points

- That failures are detected as they take place so that they can be tracked

Pay-As-You-Go Pricing

Imagine you know you want to create an online business, website, or place to store digital assets, but you have no idea where to start. You could consider buying all the hardware and software, installing, patching, maintaining, and storing it in your office. This is called a **fixed expense**. Or, you could look to the Cloud to take care of these tasks. The variable nature of Cloud computing means you can focus your budget on **variable expenses** and pay as you go, building your business in the Cloud.

Moving from fixed expenses is one of Cloud computing's core benefits. The main idea behind this shift is embracing the concept that you want to move away from large one-time purchases and instead embrace expenses  that fluctuate, based on usage. Cloud computing offers services that help you scale your expenses and manage your budget according to the way you intend to use them.

Focus on Business, Not Managing Infrastructure

Before the days of Cloud computing, if you wanted a place to store your data, run a website, and handle incoming and outgoing transactions either locally or over the Internet, you had to buy or rent your own server. You probably then had to store it somewhere cool and safe, install software that you needed to keep it up-to-date, and connect it to other servers via networks that you might have had to set up yourself.

With Cloud computing, these tasks can be out-sourced. Instead of buying your own equipment and running your own private data center, you can benefit from the huge data centers available for you.

What Are Cloud Economics?

When we talk about *Cloud economics,* what are we referring to? It's a term used to define the financial benefits and costs associated with using Cloud computing, as opposed to other ways of managing infrastructure. By moving to the Cloud, how much money is your business going to spend and, ideally, save? Quantifying the return on investment (ROI) of this method of hosting infrastructure is an important aspect of building a business that will scale.

This section quantifies the various aspects of Cloud economics and explains how they pertain to your use cases.

The Total Cost of Ownership

How much does it cost to host your business, school, or private enterprise in the Cloud? To answer this question, understanding a little vocabulary is necessary. Calculating the total cost of ownership (TCO) of your on-premises, hybrid, or Cloud infrastructure involves understanding the costs incurred to host, run, and manage the life span of your Cloud workloads. TCO in general is calculated as a sum of your initial cost and your maintenance costs, minus the asset's devaluation over time. But let's start by under-standing a few baseline concepts that impact that cost.

NOTE: You can use the handy AWS Pricing Calculator to help forecast and analyze the cost of running AWS workloads at `https://calculator.aws`.

OpEx

Operational expense (OpEx) refers to the ongoing expenses incurred when running a business. A useful example is an everyday expense that you have to pay to run a server, including the electrical bill and the bill you pay to keep the server room cool. Any rent you have to pay to keep your business up and running, such as renting the server hardware and insuring it, as well as meeting payroll and managing inventory, are all part of your OpEx. If there's an ongoing expense that's needed

to keep your organization's lights on day in and day out, that's OpEx. Your TCO is impacted by the long-term operational expenses that add up as your business grows and scales.

CapEx

Capital expense (CapEx), on the other hand, defines those large expenses that occur less regularly, such as buying a building, vehicles, or machinery to support your business. Fixed assets, often termed *property, plant, and equipment* (PP&E), are another example of CapEx. In general, consider CapEx expenses as the spending you have to do on physical assets. Your TCO is impacted immediately by CapEx purchases.

In the context of Cloud computing, it's vital to understand how your shift from an on-premises model into a Cloud model will impact your budget. **Cloud computing, with its flexible pay-as-you-go model, allows you to shift your expenses from CapEx to OpEx.** This shift will have implications for your budget forecasting and taxes, so it's important to understand the difference and how it will impact your bottom line. Managing the balance between your CapEx and OpEx costs is an important aspect of managing your budget and predicting long-term impacts to your TCO.

Labor Costs

No matter how much automation is available, there are still labor costs associated with doing business, whether in the Cloud or on-premises.

But maintaining your own data center has significant costs that can be mitigated by moving to the Cloud. To run your data center on-premises, you need to budget for a mix of CapEx and OpEx. In particular, you need staff to support and maintain the following:

- Server and network infrastructure
- Physical security
- Facility maintenance
- Climate control
- Fire suppression systems
- Backup power systems

Each business should understand the budgetary ramifications of moving their infrastructure fully or partially into the Cloud, as the labor costs shift from a more local, in-house expenditure to being attached to a data center.

Software Licensing

An important aspect of provisioning infrastructure is paying for the software license that makes them usable for the tasks required. Licenses can be tricky to manage, as they are priced according to the numbers of users and the type of hardware required. If you are creating a new environment in the Cloud, provisioning software to support it includes licensing it.

AWS supports several types of licensing models to help you better manage your software. AWS License Manager can help you manage this process.

- **BYOL:** Bring your own license. If you already own a software license, you can port it into the Cloud.
- **Granted licenses:** These licenses come with software purchased from AWS Marketplace.
- **LI:** An AWS License Included model for new environments, such as a license for Microsoft SQL Server.

The details involved in licensing can be daunting, and in an on-premises environment they are up to you to handle. By using Cloud services to handle licensing, you have more flexibility as your business grows to help your software evolve to suit.

How Can You Reduce Costs?

No business ever in the history of business has wanted, for the fun of it, to pay more than was strictly necessary for a given service. Their profitability depends on their ability to balance their costs against their revenue. So what are some tips that Cloud computing can offer to help control infrastructure costs? Let's dive in.

Right-Sizing Infrastructure

It's a gamble when setting up an on-premises server room where you have to "rack and stack" all your hardware. What if you set up an immense server room with a huge amount of compute, network, and storage, and then your business shrinks or changes in scope entirely? What if you don't buy enough hardware and your company goes viral? What if you accidentally install the wrong software on your boxes or experience a catastrophic outage causing significant down-time? Making guesses about how much stor-age and compute you need is a risky business for your business. It's better to "right-size" your infrastructure.

The right-sizing process in AWS Cloud involves making sure your capacity matches your work-loads in a granular fashion, and it's a great way to control costs. By continually watching your infra-structure for opportunities to efficiently increase or decrease capacity to match workloads, you can fine-tune your operational expenditures. By continually monitoring and enforcing a sys-tem of tagging your resources, you can right-size your infrastructure when you build it natively in the Cloud or when you move your infrastructure from on-premises into the Cloud. In this way, you avoid wasting money on unused or underused resources.

Automation

It's one thing to build an infrastructure native to the Cloud or to port your on-premises setup to the Cloud. You can take your Cloud presence to the next level by automating many steps required for its maintenance. Automation involves the execution of a process behind the scenes, either via a timer, in response to an event, or ad hoc, taking the error-prone human guesswork out of maintenance. One service that supports automation is AWS CloudFormation, designed to help manage your infrastructure using templates, automating resource management across your organization.

A good example of one type of automation is a sort of "dress rehearsal" of building, deploying, and rolling back instances of services to ensure that changes can be deployed into production seamlessly, avoiding costly downtime. Another example of this type is automating the application of patches to operating systems. You could automate scaling your systems' capacity as demand rises and falls to avoid more costly guesswork. You could also automatically deploy security improvements across the board to make sure your entire infrastructure is equally secure. You could automate the documentation of your patches, changes, and fixes to make sure they are reproducible for the next cycle, and you could make sure, via automation, that your system can recover quickly from errors, freeing you to concentrate on scaling your business, rather than worrying about manually managing the infrastructure that supports it.

Reduce Compliance Scope

One aspect of running a business is keeping in compliance with various regulations. Examples include the Health Insurance Portability and Accountability Act (HIPAA), which regulates how patient data is handled, and Payment Card

Industry Data Security Standard (PCI) compliance, which regulates the handling of credit cards. General Data Protection Regulation (GDPR) is a compliance standard required in the European Union. Making sure your business stays compliant with all these systems can be very expensive and involves extensive reporting. AWS supports more than 140 compliance standards, helping you manage your responsibilities for keeping in compliance with various tools you can use in the Cloud. Managing compliance is part of the *shared responsibility model*, which you learn about later.

Managed Services

Some AWS services offer **managed services**, which abstract away some of their complexity so that you can focus on their business value. Their infrastructure and detailed setup is taken care of behind the scenes. An example of this type of service includes the database service

DynamoDB, which hides the infrastructure setup, and the Relational Database Service (RDS) where the database engine is managed. While these services can involve higher pricing, the invisible underlying infrastructure involved in setting them up and managing them behind the scenes—which you don't have to worry about—makes adopting them a cost savings in many instances.

How Should You Design Your Cloud Architecture?

It can seem daunting to think about designing an entire Cloud architecture from scratch, but take a moment to think about all the times you've interacted with a suboptimal system on the Internet. Remember when you stared at a page on the

Web, waiting for images to download, or experienced an outage that caused you to lose work?

Outages can be catastrophic, grounding thousands of flights, or they can last just a few seconds, causing loading to stop for a short time. If you are in the business of managing a company or service that's reliant on the Internet, it's up to you to make sure you design a robust infrastructure. The following sections explain four best practices to help you do that.

Design for Failure

Outages. Everyone hates them, from customers who can't add their item to their cart to retailers who find that their sales pipeline suddenly stops flowing. How can you design your infrastructure to *expect* failure and handle failure when it happens? Failure management is part of the Reliability pillar of the *Well-Architected Framework,* which is covered in the next section. But it's also necessary to expect failures to happen and to adapt your infrastructure design to handle it well. In other words, think pessimistically and design for fault-tolerance. There are several techniques available to ensure this best practice:

- Building a **distributed architecture** that avoids single points of failure. Use multiple availability zones (covered more in Chapter 3) so that if there's a failure in one, your workload can "fail over" to another. Failures tend to be contained to single AZs.

- Make sure your data and components are **redundant**, replicated across multiple resources, using load balancers, for example, to distribute traffic across redundant resources.

- **Isolate failures** so that their impact is minimized. Use *microservices*—small, independent services you can connect to via APIs—for example, which can be designed to fail without taking down an entire system.
- Plan for disasters and for **disaster recovery**, using well-documented best practices.
- Test your system's resilience using tooling to simulate failures; this technique is called **chaos engineering**.

Decouple Components vs. Monolithic Architecture

You're going to need to understand the trade-offs between creating a monolithic versus a decoupled architecture as you plan for failure.

A **monolithic** architecture is described as one workload that does many things. It grows as business needs grow, and its processes are tightly coupled or connected. If one part of it goes down, the rest will, too.

A **decoupled** architecture can be made of many microservices, which, despite their name, aren't necessarily small. They are, instead, autonomous and specialized. Their job is to encapsulate a business capability. They should be able to be built, tested, deployed, and changed independently.

An example of a monolithic service is a service that encapsulates users, posts, and responses to posts.

A decoupled microservice architecture would split those services into three: users, posts, responses. If one goes down, the rest don't go down with it. This is good infrastructure design.

NOTE: Using AWS services such as Lambda and Amazon Elastic Containers are good choices when building a decoupled microservice architecture.

Implement Elasticity in the Cloud vs. On-Premises

The **elasticity** of Cloud computing is one of its great capabilities. If there's a sudden surge of traffic in an on-premises data center and servers go down, the failure can be much more challenging to a business than when one part of an elastic Cloud architecture fails. In an elastic, Cloud-enabled architecture, when one part fails, another part can become available as new resources are provisioned. Traffic can re-route to these new resources, and the failure is invisible to customers.

Think Parallel

Finally, it's important to think in parallel when designing your Cloud architecture. This means designing your system to be able to handle multiple requests simultaneously. Services can be paired to offload jobs to each other and ensure that the workload is handled seamlessly.

An example might be one microservice designed to intake images from hundreds of concurrent users and store them in a database, while a second service waits for a response from each upload and analyzes it for its content using machine learning. Moving away from designing sequential processes and designing instead toward a multithreaded, asynchronous architecture—for example, using a multithreaded process to put images into S3 while asynchronously reacting to each put—will improve its speed and reliability.

The Well-Architected Framework

There's a useful *mental model* called the Well-Architected Framework that can help you design and operate your business systems in the Cloud. This framework sets you up for success by helping you understand the pros and cons of decisions you have to make while building in the Cloud. It is divided into six sections or pillars, and it's really helpful to understand these well as core concepts for the Cloud practitioner to master. The following sections discuss these pillars.

Pillar 1: Operational Excellence

The Operational Excellence pillar is about improvement, not only of technology but also about people and processes. You should be able to run your workloads, learn about how well or poorly they operate, and improve them throughout their lifecycle. Check out this pillar's five design principles:

- **Operations as code:** You can design your whole infrastructure using version-controlled code, which allows you to update it more easily and use it for automating operational procedures.

- **Frequent, small changes:** Design your workloads so that you can update them frequently with the ability to reverse your changes without issues.
- **Frequent refinements:** Small, incremental changes help you refine your procedures gradually.
- **Anticipate failure:** In life, optimism is great, but in infrastructure and application code, it's better to expect the worst and be ready to learn from failures. You can set up tests to see how well your workloads and your team respond to disasters.
- **Learn from failures:** Also as in life, share what you learned from your failures across your team and your organization so the same mistake won't be made twice!

Pillar 2: Security

A key aspect of AWS Cloud computing is its high emphasis on security. This pillar focuses on protecting information and systems. It's important for customers to be sure that their data and infrastructure are secure. Moving to the Cloud, in fact, can act as a means to enhance security. These seven principles outline how security is handled in the AWS Cloud:

- **Implement a strong identity policy:** This means using the *principle of least privilege*, meaning that you ensure that each element of your architecture has appropriate authorization policies in place.

- **Enable traceability:** Make sure you can trace any changes or events in your architecture by capturing logs and metrics.

- **Apply security at all layers:** Each layer of your architecture should have multiple security controls.

- **Automate security:** Use software to manage your security seamlessly.

- **Protect data in transit and data at rest:** Understand the various ways your data moves through your system and protect it by classifying it according to sensitivity. This is a good opportunity to use encryption to protect data in transit and access management for data at rest.

- **Keep people away from data:** Human error can often cause security incidents, so use tools to avoid the need to manipulate data manually.

- **Prepare for security events:** Expect the best, but prepare for the worst. Make sure your systems are ready for incidents and run simulations to make sure that such problems can be detected, investigated, and recovered from.

Pillar 3: Reliability

Reliability in the Cloud means that workloads are monitored for their availability and they can recover from disruptions. A reliable system also has tests to determine and mitigate potential points of failure. Agility, elasticity, and scalability also factor in to ensure the reliability of a system, and these aspects can all be automated to reduce human error. A good example of a reliable system is one where when one component sees a spike in demand—a video goes viral, for example—an automation adds resources to support this additional load and removes the resources when the load goes down.

The Reliability pillar includes these five design principles:

- **Automatic recovery:** Use automation to monitor your workloads and trigger a notification and recovery process to repair a failure.
- **Testable procedures:** Make sure your recovery procedures are solid by setting up tests to simulate failures and recovery solutions.
- **Horizontal scaling:** Instead of having one large resource, use many smaller resources in your architecture so that failures won't impact such a large area.
- **Elastic capacity:** When demand exceeds supply, automate expanding or removal of resources.
- **Automated changes:** Use automation as well to make changes to your infrastructure.

Pillar 4: Performance Efficiency

When we talk about performance efficiency, we're referring to using your available resources in the most efficient way to meet your workload's requirements. Performance has to do with a system's response speed and use of memory. This efficiency needs to keep up with any changes in your system's demand and any changes in technology, as well. This pillar includes these five principles:

- **Democratize technology:** Let AWS take care of managing complex tasks in the Cloud, rather than asking in-house staff to manage it. This way, you can focus on your business needs and your customer's experience.

- **Go global in minutes:** Deploy your workloads around the world using multiple AWS Regions. Your customers will appreciate the lower latency and faster service.

NOTE   **AWS Regions** are physical locations around the world that hold a cluster of data centers that host AWS resources. Inside each region there are at least three Availability Zones, discussed in Chapter 3.

- **Go serverless:** Using serverless technologies means you don't have to maintain physical servers or manage and pay for physical server operations.

NOTE: **Serverless** means using architectures that remove the need for servers—an S3 storage bucket instead of a web server, for example.

- **Experiment!** With your Cloud environment, you can test and experiment to see what configurations work best.
- **Consider mechanical sympathy:** This is a fancy way to say "Use the tool that's right for

the job." For example, use a NoSQL database when it makes sense over a relational database.

Pillar 5: Cost Optimization

The Cost Optimization pillar is all about—you guessed it—delivering the highest value at the lowest price point. Learn how to save money by following these five design principles:

- **Invest in knowledge:** Make sure that your business is well equipped to make good decisions to optimize cost.

- **Adopt a consumption model:** While you might be tempted to forecast how much compute you might need, it's better to lean on the elasticity of the Cloud and increase and decrease usage proactively to save.

- **Measure efficiency:** Knowledge is power, so measure and keep track of your costs and savings as you increase and decrease compute, networking, storage, and governance.

- **Stop spending money on IT infrastructure:** Let AWS do that for you! You don't need to rack and stack your own data centers if you've invested in the Cloud, just like you don't need to construct your own tent if a ready-made one is available.

- **Analyze:** Identify which elements of your workloads are consuming so you can know where to optimize them to reduce costs and attribute those costs to the appropriate people running them.

Pillar 6: Sustainability

According to the United Nations, sustainable development is "development that meets the needs of the present without compromising the ability of future generations to meet their own needs." In this spirit, this sixth pillar of the Well-Architected Framework includes the goal of helping make organizations more sustainable via reducing the harms that infrastructure can cause to our environment.

Take a look at these best practices:

- **Understand the impact:** Know the impact of your workloads on the environment so that you can target inefficient ones and make their impact less harmful.
- **Establish goals:** Establish sustainability goals and work toward meeting them on a timeline that works for you.
- **Maximize utilization:** Fewer resources that are utilized at a higher percentage are more efficient than more workloads that are less utilized.

- **Adopt efficient hardware and software:** Be aware and ready to implement more efficient services that become available to you.
- **Use managed services:** When many customers share workloads, they are more efficient, so prioritize shared, managed services.
- **Reduce downstream impact:** Constantly upgrading devices (like the one you used to reserve your campground) causes environmental impact, so make sure your infrastructure can be used on current devices, continually testing to ensure their compatibility.

CHAPTER TWO

Staying Safe with Security and Compliance

Welcome to Chapter 2. In this chapter, you learn how to make sure you're building in the Cloud using safe processes with security and compliance well in hand. Specifically, this chapter covers the following topics:

- The shared responsibility model
- Security and compliance concepts
- Access management capabilities
- AWS Identity and Access Management (IAM)
- Identifying resources for security support

By the end of this chapter, you will know how to keep security and compliance top of mind as you journey into the Cloud. Let's get started!

Introduction

It shouldn't be a surprise that security and compliance are "job zero" at Amazon, making customer safety the main priority. AWS builds services to help achieve security and compliance, and it builds these practices into their other services. After all, millions of users entrust the AWS Cloud every second with details about their bank information, personal data, shopping preferences, and more.

NOTE: **Security** refers to the processes and technologies used to secure sensitive data, systems, and assets, while **compliance** refers to your adherence to regulatory standards to align with contractual or legal requirements.

When on a camping trip, you make sure that safety and security play an important role as you plan the trip's details. You lock your camper's doors, for example, as a security practice. You make sure to store your food in bear-proof containers and practice fire safety, ensuring that you extinguish your fire properly once your meal is done. You also make sure you have a valid pass to use the campground where you've reserved a spot and abide by local rules. By following best practices in the Cloud, you will similarly ensure that your data is transmitted and stored safely, your assets are secure, and your systems are in compliance. Let's discover some of these practices together.

The Shared Responsibility Model

What is shared responsibility? It's the concept that you, as the Cloud practitioner, and AWS share the responsibility to keep systems secure and compliant. But where is that fine line between "mine" and "theirs" drawn?

In general, AWS's responsibility is security **of** the Cloud while the customer's responsibility is security **in** the Cloud. This might come as a bit of a relief to someone who is used to handling all the security and compliance of an on-premises data center, but it also merits careful consideration since these responsibilities vary depending on the services used. These services are defined as falling into one of three categories: infrastructure as a service (IaaS), platform as a service (PaaS), and software as a service (SaaS). Services fall into these categories depending on their level of *abstraction*—how much visibility the customer has into their inner workings.

NOTE: In general, the more abstraction, the more responsibility falls on AWS for security and compliance.

Let's examine the shared responsibility model and look at a few examples of how the line is drawn between the customer's responsibility and that of AWS, depending on the type of service.

The Customer's Responsibility

If the customer is responsible for security **in** the Cloud, what does that mean, practically speaking? Consider three examples of services that you might select: EC2, Lambda, and RDS.

- **Amazon EC2**, or Elastic Compute Cloud, is an example of *infrastructure as a service*. It is a *virtualized* device, meaning you deploy software onto the instance that acts the same as software you'd install on a physical device. This means you are responsible for the security of the software that you deploy onto this instance, just as you would have been on a physical device. Any security patches or updates needed by the software or operating systems that you virtualize on this instance need to be made secure and compliant by you. AWS, however, is responsible for the security of the underlying EC2 infrastructure itself, so you're not flying completely solo!

- **Amazon Lambda** is a serverless compute solution that "hides" the server from the customer. In this way it qualifies as a *platform as a service* that allows you to run code in response to certain events, such as when an order is placed and a push notification needs to be sent to the client. Because Lambda lets you run code that you write as Lambda functions, it's your job to ensure that the code is secure and compliant. But AWS will ensure that the underlying infrastructure, operating system, and application platform powering Lambda are kept up-to-date in terms of security. It's on you to maintain the security of your code.

- **AWS Relational Database Service** (RDS) is a service that allows you to set up a relational database in the Cloud. It lets you install your favorite relational database—such as Maria DB, Microsoft SQL Server, Oracle, PostgreSQL, or MySQL—on top of AWS-managed infrastructure. Like the previously mentioned services, the shared responsibility model of RDS means you are responsible for the security of the databases that you install on RDS. It's also up to you to manage the username and password strategies, often with tools such as IAM or AWS Secrets Manager. You use the tools provided by RDS to ensure that your data is secure. AWS will ensure that the infrastructure underlying RDS is secure and compliant.

NOTE: You could say that while AWS is responsible for the database, the customer is responsible for the data and the access to it.

AWS's Responsibility

Now that you know that AWS's responsibility lies in making every element **of** the AWS Cloud safe, secure, and compliant, let's think about how this actually works. AWS takes responsibility for the security and compliance of the infrastructure **of** the Cloud, including its hardware, software, and networking.

One of the best-known AWS services—Simple Storage Service (**S3**)—offers an infrastructure layer, operating systems, and platforms with which customers can interact. AWS ensures the security of these aspects of the service, and customers manage the security and compliance of their data, its encryption, and IAM permissions to ensure proper permissions are assigned to the various assets stored on S3.

NOTE: It's worthwhile to note that compliance regulations can vary region to region. A good example is GDPR, which regulates how data is stored in Europe. You need to understand and act on the ramifications of storing data in a region with specific regulations.

Table 2.1 outlines the shared responsibility model.

Table 2.1 The Shared Responsibility Model

On-Premises	IaaS	PaaS	SaaS
Applications	*Applications*	*Applications*	**Applications**
Customer data	*Customer data*	*Customer data*	**Customer data**
Runtime	*Runtime*	**Runtime**	**Runtime**
Middleware	*Middleware*	**Middleware**	**Middleware**
Operating system	*Operating system*	**Operating system**	**Operating system**
Virtualization	**Virtualization**	**Virtualization**	**Virtualization**
Networking	**Networking**	**Networking**	**Networking**
Storage	**Storage**	**Storage**	**Storage**
Servers	**Servers**	**Servers**	**Servers**

Note: Italics indicates the user/customer responsibility. Bold indicates the provider responsibility.

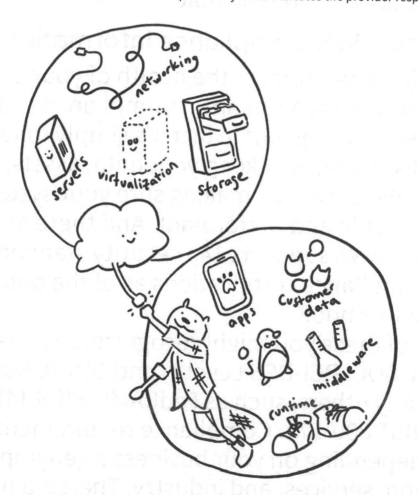

Security and Compliance Concepts

This next section looks at security and compliance, which relate to each other like making sure that the brakes on your camper work *and* ensuring that you've passed all your emissions inspections before hitting the road!

Finding AWS Compliance Information

Security is essential to the health of your business, and so is compliance. Compliance sounds like a scary thing, but in fact it's simply following established rules to keep your data, assets, and code safe, as well as making sure your systems are available and performant. And there are lots of rules! AWS supports 143 security standards and compliance certifications as of the publication of this book.

Some of these you might recognize, such as HIPAA, SOC, PCI-DSS Level 1, and GDPR. But there are many others, such as FedRAMP, FIPS 140-2, and NIST 800-171. Compliance requirements vary depending on your business's geographic location, services, and industry. There's a handy

Compliance Programs web page at `https://aws.amazon.com/compliance/programs`, where you can read about the various compliance programs available per region.

It's important to note that compliance requirements vary among the AWS services. Depending on your customer's data, where it's gathered and located, and how you are using it, you need to ensure compliance using the appropriate program by region. Visit the Services in Scope page to check the services covered by a given compliance program: `https://aws.amazon.com/compliance/services-in-scope`.

It's also worth noting that compliance is part of the shared responsibility model. AWS takes care of the compliance and security posture in the services themselves, but it is up to you to ensure that the data you manage via AWS services is used and stored in a compliant way.

NOTE: **AWS Artifact** provides free on-demand access to compliance reports and other internal AWS documents to demonstrate to auditors that the AWS offerings used meet security and compliance standards, as well as educate team members adhering to these standards.

How Can You Achieve Compliance on AWS?

So, it's up to you to make sure your AWS use remains compliant. Just how do you plan to do that? A good way to think about keeping your use of data in compliance is to plan according to the concepts of *data in transit* and *data at rest*. The most common way to handle the safe transit and storage of data is to encrypt it. All AWS services offer the ability to encrypt data at rest and in transit. This is part of the concept of **data sovereignty**—the idea that you have control over your customer data, where it's stored, who has access, and how it's encrypted.

> **NOTE:** **Encryption** is the process of encoding data so that it can be decrypted only by use of a key that's controlled by an authorized person or resource.

Who Enables Encryption on an AWS Service?

Data encryption is available in more than 100 AWS services. Data in transit can be encrypted using a certificate management service such as **AWS Certificate Manager (ACM)**, which offers public and private certificate management to ensure your data's encryption. Encryption in transit is accomplished using SSL/TLS—the *s* in your

HTTPS-enabled website refers to its encryption using SSL. The certificates needed to ensure proper encryption can be created and stored in ACM.

Data in transit can be encrypted on any layer used to transport data.

- **Network traffic** is transparently encrypted at the physical layer.

- When using supported EC2 instance types, **traffic within and between peered VPCs** is transparently encrypted at the network layer.

- You can choose to encrypt data in transit at the **application layer** between peered VPCs using SSL/TLS, which is supported by all AWS service endpoints.

When data comes to "rest," what happens? **AWS Key Management Service (KMS)** is a flexible service for data at rest that enables you to manage the encryption keys in your systems. KMS-managed keys are used to encrypt the data stored by services such as S3 and databases such as RDS.

Services That Help with Auditing and Reporting

The transactions that occur as your data moves through its lifecycle can be recorded in log files. These services can help you audit and monitor your systems by watching and analyzing what happens in your systems:

- **AWS Config** helps you determine where you're not in compliance by representing your resources' ideal configuration and detecting any noncompliance. You can then dig into problem areas.

- **AWS Audit Manager** continually audits your AWS usage to help assess compliance.

- **AWS CloudWatch** monitors (watches!) your infrastructure and the applications you run on it. It monitors logs, metrics, and alarms, making sure your application is running as expected.

- **AWS CloudTrail**, like a trail of breadcrumbs, records user activities and API calls for your account, filters logs, and records any unusual activity.

NOTE: Fun fact! AWS services record 600 billion auditing API events every day.

The Concept of Least Privileged Access

It may seem counterintuitive to think that you should grant the fewest permissions necessary when building a system that you hope will be used by millions of users. This is where the concept of *least privileged access* comes in. When creating a system such as an S3 bucket for uploads or a DynamoDB table, consider its use and who will be using it and grant permissions accordingly. If a user won't need to write to the database, make sure you enable only Read access for this type of user. As your system matures, you can make edits to the permissions associated with your system using **AWS Identity and Access Management (IAM)** tools.

AWS Access Management Capabilities

This section dives into an important aspect of security: managing who can access what in your business systems. It discusses how AWS resources access other resources. We dig into using services such as IAM to help resources access each other or, behind the scenes, to authorize users to access resources.

The Purpose of User and Identity Management

When you first sign into the AWS console using an email and password, you do so as a root user. This user has access to all the services in the account and shouldn't be used for every-day tasks. We'll come back to this point, but first let's talk about managing identity in your systems. You read about the concept of least-privileged access, but let's dive deeper. You need to be able to manage access for every entity that touches your system to guarantee its security.

You do that by managing their "identity," creating users, groups of users, and roles. These identities are associated with policies that control **what** actions a given identity can perform, **how** they can perform these actions, and **where** the actions can be performed. An example is a single user associated with a Campers group who can upload images of their campsite to a specific camp-related S3 bucket.

Access Keys and Passwords

How does one resource go about accessing another AWS resource? In general, a resource has two keys to their castle: one is an access key, and the other is a secret key, which acts like a username and password. It's part of the shared responsibility model to keep these keys safe—AWS provides safeguards so that they are not leaked, but you should avoid similar actions (don't expose an access key on GitHub, for example). To protect these keys, it's recommended that you rotate them frequently. The AWS documentation includes a series of steps you can take to avoid disruption as you rotate your credentials. You also create credentials for the users that you create in your systems. You have control over the complexity of those passwords, and you can revoke access at any time by removing passwords and access keys.

Multifactor Authentication

You've created your AWS account and signed in as the root user, so what's next? You need to activate multifactor authentication (MFA) for your root user. In the console, you can activate MFA for all sign-ins. This process allows you to connect an MFA-enabled device, such as an authentication app on your cell phone, to your account. The process of connecting your device will allow you to leverage a QR code that you scan or a secret key to connect the device to your account. Make sure to keep those items in a safe place in case you need to lose your device or it becomes disconnected. Leveraging MFA is a best practice that helps you further secure your root user's credentials and any IAM user associated with your account long-term.

Tasks That Require Root Accounts
As you saw earlier, when you create an AWS resource, you create what's called a *root user*.

This identity is protected by a password, and you need to ensure that you keep that password safe.

WARNING: Use your root user only to create an administrative user who will perform daily tasks and tasks that only a root user can do, such as closing an AWS account or restoring IAM user permissions.

There are some specific tasks that require root accounts. Otherwise, you would rely on administrative users and other less-powerful users. Some of these include the following:

- Changing account settings
- Restoring IAM user permissions
- Activating IAM access to manage billing and cost management
- Viewing some tax invoices and closing your AWS account
- Configuring an S3 bucket to enable MFA
- Tasks associated with AWS GovCloud management

View a full list at `https://docs.aws.amazon.com/accounts/latest/reference/root-user-tasks.html`.

Protecting Root Accounts

Your root account access is an important thing to protect. As with all passwords, you must follow these best practices to ensure your password stays private:

- Enable MFA.
- Don't share your password and access keys.
- Use a strong password.

WARNING: Don't create an access key for your AWS account root user. Better safe than sorry!

AWS Identity and Access Management

IAM allows you to specify who (what human) or what (what service) can access the various resources that you cre- ate in your account. The AWS docs say it per- fectly: "You use IAM to control who is authen- ticated (signed in)

and authorized (has permissions) to use resources."

Users, Roles, and Groups

Consider the case of campers who arrive at a campsite and are part of a Camping Club that allows members to use the campsite's facilities. First, they must show their ID and membership card at the gate, where the ranger authenticates their identity. Once authenticated, they are authorized by means of their membership to use the electricity, water, and firepits. If their membership expires, they no longer have access to these amenities. In the same way, IAM handles requests made by principals (IAM users, federated users from third-party providers like Google, and AWS accounts and services) and allows or denies access, based on the principal's permissions.

So far, you learned about signing in to your AWS account as a root user. Once your root user has MFA access set up, your next step is to create an administrative user so that you can avoid using the root user's credentials for anything not required for the root user to perform. This administrative user will have special "powers" that are above and beyond those of other users, however. So from this point forward, your job is to configure your systems according to the least-privilege practice discussed earlier. What's the least amount of access you need to give your users as you set them up?

NOTE: Use IAM and, specifically, IAM Access Analyzer to analyze the access policies associated with your account.

Consider a real-world use case that illustrates the interplay between users, groups, and roles. Imagine you create a DynamoDB database to store reviews of campsites. You also set up a machine learning process that needs to have read-only access to this database to mine for sentiment (negative and positive reviews). How would you handle identity to manage permissions for this use case?

A camp ranger needs access to the AWS Console to view this database, so they need an IAM user setup with minimum permissions to read the reviews in this database. The ML process running behind the scenes needs this read-only access as well. This is a great moment to use an IAM role to enable the appropriate entities to assume the role of database reader.

Now imagine that a camp auditor wants temporary access to view the reviews. You can assign them temporary use of this read-only role so that they can access the database temporarily. Finally, you might want to group all these users into a user group, perhaps called ReadOnlyCampers, which is a collection of IAM users who share the same permissions granted to all the users in this group. Once the auditor no longer needs access to read this data, you can remove them from the group.

NOTE: If you are managing identity outside of AWS or across AWS accounts, you can use IAM Identity Center with identity federation to manage their access. This is a good option

when you want to manage human access (or workforce users).

Policies

When embarking on your creation of users and the assignment of roles, you need an important tool in your toolkit: policies. **Policies** are documents that can be attached to an identity (IAM users, user groups, or roles) to specify what it can do, or to a resource (such as an S3 bucket) to specify what can be done to it and by whom. They are stored as JSON documents. These documents allow AWS to check permissions on a given resource before giving access.

NOTE: JavaScript Object Notation (JSON) can look like this:

```
{
    "Version": "2012-10-17",
    "Statement": {
      "Effect": "Allow",
      "Action": "s3:ListBucket",
      "Resource": "arn:aws:s3:::camp_reviews_bucket"
    }
}
```

A common way to use a policy is to attach it to an identity in IAM. To do this, you use a managed, inline, or custom policy.

- **AWS-managed policies:** A stand-alone policy created by AWS that takes the guesswork out of assigning permissions. You don't have to write it yourself, but you also can't edit it. AWS also handles updates that keep permissions up-to-date for resources using these policies.

- **Customer-managed policies:** Stand-alone polices that can be attached to principals. You can edit these whenever needed, and all the changes will propagate to the principal entities where the policy is attached.

- **Inline:** Can be coupled to a single IAM identity so that when you delete an identity, you also delete its policy. It specifies the permissions for only that identity.

TIP: A smart way to create a customized policy is to copy an existing one and alter it.

Identifying Resources for Security Support

Security is so important, and yet so daunting, that it's comforting to know you have some choices to help you manage your resources' security needs. Some come from AWS itself, some from third parties on the AWS Marketplace.

Getting Help with Security

Use this list to discover a few strategies to help you manage your business system security. A list of AWS services that help manage security is available at `https://aws.amazon.com/products/security`.

- Enable AWS Security Hub for your account so that you can see security vulnerabilities and how they align to affected resources. Use Security Hub to mitigate any issues it finds. Security Hub offers a complete view of your security state, helping you compare your current setup with industry standards.

- If you are managing a website's security, set up a firewall using the Web Application Firewall (WAF), which protects your website from attacks, such as SQL injections and cross-site scripting (XSS), as well as monitors incoming traffic. Use AWS Trusted Advisor's console to audit any findings from AWS Security Hub.

- Use Amazon GuardDuty to analyze data sources, checking for any malicious activity and compromised instances.

- Use AWS Shield to watch for distributed denial-of-service (DDoS) attacks.

- Use Amazon Inspector for continual, automated scanning of your environments that checks for software vulnerabilities.

- Align to the AWS Well-Architected Security pillar's best practices: `https://docs.aws.amazon.com/wellarchitected/latest/security-pillar/welcome.html`.

- Leverage third-party security products from the AWS Marketplace to enhance your security: `https://aws.amazon.com/marketplace/solutions/security`.

Security Documentation

Once again, when security is in question, you don't walk alone! There is a considerable amount of documentation about this important topic. Note the following in particular:

- **AWS Knowledge Center:** `https://repost.aws/knowledge-center` is a repository of useful official articles that answer the most frequently asked questions about AWS.

- **Security Center:** The main repository of security information on AWS's documentation is at `https://aws.amazon.com/security`. You can learn how to raise your security posture here.

- **AWS Security blog:** Find articles at `https://aws.amazon.com/security/blogs` about how various customers and partners manage and enhance their security, as well as pertinent service announcements.

- **Partner Systems Integrators:** Visit AWS's Marketplace to learn about third-party security solutions at `https://aws.amazon.com/marketplace/solutions/security` and the Partner Security Resources page to learn more about partner security implementation options at `https://aws.amazon.com/security/partner-resources`.

- **Well-Architected Security Pillar:** We covered this in Chapter 1, but don't forget the best practices covered at `https://docs.aws.amazon.com/wellarchitected/latest/security-pillar/welcome.html`.

AWS Trusted Advisor

AWS Trusted Advisor is a service that's all about helping you follow best practices, including those focusing on your security posture by providing automated checks. Trusted Advisor will check your account's security no matter your level of support.

If you subscribe to. . .

- **AWS Developer Support**, you can use Trusted Advisor to access core security checks and service quota checks.

- **AWS Business or Enterprise Support**, you can access all checks offered by Trusted Advisor, including cost optimization, performance, security, fault tolerance, and service quotas.

NOTE: AWS Trusted Advisor Priority is available to Enterprise Support customers, providing prioritized and context-driven recommendations as well as the standard suite of security checks.

CHAPTER THREE

Entering the Cloud

Welcome to Chapter 3. Now that you've learned some basic Cloud computing concepts and are confident in your knowledge about security and compliance in the AWS Cloud, it's time to start your camper's engine and hit the road. In this chapter, you learn about the following:

- Deploying to and operating in the AWS Cloud
- Different ways of provisioning and operating in the AWS Cloud
- Identifying connectivity options

By the end of this chapter, you will be able to identify the various ways that you can build your business in the Cloud. Let's get started!

Introduction

So far, you've been packing your bags and preparing to build in the AWS Cloud by carefully considering security and compliance as well as identity, with an overview of users, groups, and roles driven by IAM. Now, it's time to get a little bit closer to your goal of working with the various services that AWS offers in the Cloud so you can realize your business and personal goals. Let's get ready to go!

Different Ways of Provisioning and Operating in the AWS Cloud

So, you want to access the AWS Cloud? There are several ways to do that. You can use the many tools available to manage your infrastructure. Let's take a look at some of your options.

- **Programmatic access:** Get programmatic access to AWS services from within by leveraging one of the tools made available to you, including APIs, SDKs, and CLI commands.
  - **APIs:** Most services, like EC2, allow access via an API. You can make HTTP requests to GET or POST data to your EC2 instance, provided you are authenticated.
  - **SDKs:** Purpose-built software development kits (SDKs) allow you to access your AWS services using a supported programming language. In general, it's recommended that developers leverage SDKs that use APIs under the hood to provide language-specific APIs for AWS services.

- ○ **CLIs:** You can use command-line interfaces (CLIs) in Windows, in Linux, on a physical server, or on a Mac. They are a way to interact with AWS services by issuing CLI commands. While AWS has its own CLI that supports each AWS service, some services also have their own CLI. Use the AWS CLI when you want to create and use scripts to perform operations on multiple AWS services and when you prefer to use the command line over a graphical interface.

- **AWS Management Console:** This is a web interface that gives you access to all the AWS services you need to run your business. The Management Console lets you search for services that you can quickly try, often for free using the free tier (remember, the free tier varies per service). It's also useful to quickly check the configuration of a service. You can also get quick access to account and billing dashboards, documentation, and support from the AWS Console. In general, however, when setting up production workloads, use infrastructure as code.

- **Infrastructure as code (IaC):** Provision your infrastructure by writing code, instead of using manual scripts and runbooks. IaC helps you provision your infrastructure by writing deployable code templates. It's better to use this technique, rather than using manual methods such as the Management Console. By using this technique, central to AWS's DevOps principles, you can centralize your provisioning system, storing it in source control. AWS CloudFormation offers a helpful way to write and maintain your IaC templates.

Types of Deployment Models

Generally speaking, there are three obvious routes to deploying your resources and work-loads into the AWS Cloud. You can deploy your apps and workloads via services in the AWS Cloud. Alternately, you can manage on-premises serv-ers, where you have direct control over your infrastruc-ture and data. Or you can deploy to a hybrid model, which includes both public and private deployment models, where you can connect your on-premises infrastructure to the Cloud

when appropriate. Let's take a look at some examples where using one of these three models might work.

"All In" the Cloud

The best-known method of deploying your applications and hosting your data is in the Cloud, that vast array of servers managed by AWS. All different kinds of systems can all be run in the Cloud. Rather like a campsite, AWS offers a managed space where you can rent a space and pitch your tent. If AWS provides the campground, an electrical hookup, and a fire pit, you have to rent your space in it, build your own fire, and bring food to cook.

Thousands of customers worldwide share these server allocations in "Camp AWS." The Cloud offers cost savings to customers who want to outsource their IT costs. Following the shared responsibility model, they thus can offload some costs and burdens of managing infrastructure onto a third-party provider like AWS. Of course, they do need to ensure that they uphold their part of the shared responsibility model and ensure that their own customer's data remains accessible only to those who have the proper permissions.

Hybrid Model

In some circumstances, you might choose to deploy your workloads onto a combination of provider types. In this infrastructure design, you integrate internal resources with a third-party Cloud provider's infrastructure and resources, forming a whole infrastructure of disparate parts.

There are some interesting benefits to building a hybrid Cloud. If you are hosting some data that needs special care to ensure it is in compliance, for example, you might host that on-premises and connect it to the Cloud to control its access. You can also depend on the Cloud to handle extra traffic spikes that might occur on the on-premises servers. You can also depend on one Cloud to perform as a backup for the other, ensuring redundancy and resiliency.

Of course, this infrastructure model is more complicated and requires more specialized knowledge to maintain.

On-Premises Model

In an on-premises model, you are responsible for acquiring and installing your own software on your own on-premises data centers. You'll need an IT department to manage all the infra-structure your business needs, and you'll need to purchase and maintain your software and hardware, making sure to update it and configure it properly for your needs. Managing all this on your own can be complex, but fortunately AWS offers specific services made to operate in this type of environment, such as AWS Outposts, which allows you to extend and run native AWS services on-premises.

NOTE: You can also use an architecture called a **private Cloud**, which in this context means a computing environment dedicated to just one organization, such as your company's intranet. Read more on this distinction at `https://aws .amazon.com/what-is/private-cloud`. There are three types of private Clouds.

- On-premises private Cloud, managed by your organization including all software and hardware management
- Managed private Cloud, managed by a third-party provider
- Virtual private Cloud, an isolated environment within the Cloud

Considering Migration Options

At some point in your Cloud journey, you may decide that you need to migrate your workloads into the Cloud or into some alternate infrastructure model. How do you do that? You might start by consulting the Cloud Adoption Framework (CAF) at `https://aws.amazon.com/cloud-adoption-framework`. This is a useful model to assess each of these model's pros and cons, including reduced business risk, environmental, social, and governance ramifications, revenue trade-offs, and operational efficiencies.

Take the Cloud Readiness Assessment to assess your business's priorities and readiness to migrate. Then, if you decide to take the plunge, learn about the migration strategies at the AWS Migration Hub at `https://aws.amazon.com/migration-hub`. This hub outlines steps you can take to discover and import information about your current infrastructure, build a plan for migration, and then, if applicable, use the migration orchestrator to help rehost applications and re-platform databases. Depending on what your current needs are and how you want to import them into a Cloud environment, there are tools listed to help you achieve your goals.

Identifying Connectivity Options

Now that you've learned about the types of environments to which you can deploy your workloads and applications, let's discuss how you can connect to the Cloud.

VPN

You might already be familiar with a virtual private network (VPN) as a link between your computer and your office's network.

  VPNs are used to connect your computer or that of your staff (in office or remote) to the Cloud or to connect on-premises infrastructure to Cloud infrastructure.

- AWS offers an elastic **Client VPN** that connects users to a VPN endpoint via a free software package that users use to connect their on-premises computer to either the AWS Cloud or your on-premises network.

- The AWS **Site-to-Site VPN** connects sites such as your office network to the Cloud using an encrypted link. The connection is made when a configuration file is downloaded to your device or router, nego-tiating a secure connection to the server.

AWS Direct Connect

AWS Direct Connect offers a way for you to connect your Internet network to AWS over a fiberoptic Ethernet cable. Because it's the shortest pathway between you and your AWS resources, it also reduces latency.

> **NOTE:**   **Latency**, in this context, refers to the delay between sending and receiving data. Remember when you were a kid and strung two tin cans together with string to create a telephone? Maybe you noticed that when the cord was shorter, communication was easier and clearer. Signals that travel shorter distances have lower latency, or less of a delay.

You connect one end to the router and the other to an AWS Direct Connect router. In this way, you can avoid the public Internet by creating this direct connection. You might, for example, use it to connect your on-premises data center to a microservice hosted in the AWS Cloud.

Public Internet

If you've decided that you want to use the public Internet to connect your device or office to the Cloud, what does that entail? First, you need to ensure that the assets on the Cloud that you need to be connected can be reached via the Internet.

A tool you can use to do this is a virtual private cloud (VPC). This is a virtual network that acts as a standard network but operates in the Cloud, rather than locally. Your AWS account comes provisioned with default VPCs, and, depending on the complexity of your network needs, you would use roughly the following path to get connected:

1. Create a **VPC** in your account or use an existing one.
2. Add a **subnet**, a range of IP addresses available within one Availability Zone (more on this later).
3. Deploy your AWS resources in your new VPC.

NOTE: Not all AWS resources go in a VPC. DynamoDB, S3, API Gateway, and many others do not go in a VPC. EC2, Elastic Load Balancer, RDS, and ElastiCache are examples of AWS resources that *do* go inside a VPC.

4. Assign public **IP addresses** to the various resources in your VPC from the subnets you defined, for example, an IP address for an EC2 instance.
5. Create a **route table** to show where traffic from your subnets should be directed.
6. Use an **Internet gateway** to connect your VPC to the Internet.

7. If necessary, use a **VPC peering connection** to route traffic between two VPCs.

8. Monitor traffic and capture logs using traffic monitoring software and VPC flow logs.

9. Connect your VPC to your office's **VPN** to connect securely to the Internet.

Going Global

The previous section discussed how to connect your devices to the Internet, but the Internet is a very big, interconnected place with a lot of traffic! It doesn't make much sense to have your office in Boston constantly accessing data in Tokyo if you want to reduce latency. How can the Cloud help you ensure that your infrastructure aligns to the best well-architected practices for resilience in a distributed world?

The AWS Cloud offers a useful model to understand how the elastic Cloud can expand across regions so that you can take your business from local to global. Let's dive into the concept of Regions, Availability Zones, and Edge Locations.

Staying Highly Available with Availability Zones

It's likely that, when running an online workload, you need it to be *resilient*—online for as much time as needed—which includes being highly available and able to recover from disasters with as low latency as possible. How do you ensure this high availability?

The answer is by using multiple Availability Zones. As of this book's writing, there are 32 global regions with 99 Availability Zones scattered through these regions. According to AWS, "an Availability Zone (AZ) is one or more discrete data centers with redundant power, networking, and connectivity in an AWS Region." Deploying your workload in US-East-1, a region in Northern Virginia, for example, offers six AZs into which you can partition your applications. All the AZs in a region are located a meaningful distance (many kilometers) from another regional AZ, so they are separate enough to withstand a tornado, lightning strikes, floods, or other natural disasters that might affect one data center in an AZ. They are designed to be fault-tolerant and highly available, and they are connected to each other via an encrypted, low-latency network.

TIP: Leveraging the benefits of AZs will normally satisfy most demand for low-latency highly available applications in the Cloud. You'll be well covered to provision redundant resources in several AZs so that if there is a failure, another AZ can take over. But if you need extremely low latency to your end users, you can use **AWS Local Zones**. Local Zones allow you to place your compute, storage, and database (for selected services) close to your customers if they are located near well-populated areas. A different service, AWS Wavelength Zones, extends a service called **AWS Wavelength** that allows developers to build ultra-low

latency applications to mobile devices by using 5G networks. Wavelength Zones are an extension of an AWS Region where a carrier is located and where Wavelength is deployed.

A Multiregion Strategy

As mentioned, there are more than 30 global regions, each consisting of multiple Availability Zones. This makes each region fault-tolerant, able to withstand a local disaster or outage. But there might be reasons you'd want to expand your reach and deploy into several regions globally.

- **Global audience reach:** At some point, you might have built a truly global business and want your customer in London to have just as speedy an experience as your customer in Tokyo. For this situation, you can create a multiregion deployment. Once your business goes global, you will want to reduce latency for your customers worldwide so that your customers in Tokyo can have a low-latency experience by accessing services and data closer to them.

- **Disaster recovery:** As your business grows, you need to enhance your disaster recovery plan to ensure that your workloads are fault-tolerant no matter the size or impact of the event. Part of this plan will include two important metrics: recovery point objective (RPO) and recovery time objective (RTO). These are your baseline acceptable amounts of downtime and loss of data in case of a disaster event. You want to keep at or below your RTO and RPO targets.

- **Local regulations:** On occasion, data can't leave a region. Consider sensitive government data or the need for a company to ensure that their  users' data remains in the same region as their users. You need to design systems where the data kept in a given region is in line with local rules and regulations, all part of a multiregion deployment strategy.

Living on the Edge

So far, you've learned about the various locations where you might want to run your AWS work-flows in the Cloud. Let's turn the discussion to the data closest to your users, the *user-facing* data. In a continual quest to improve latency for your customers as they interact with your data and assets, the concept of *edge networking* comes in handy. Edge can move traffic from the Internet onto the AWS backbone and redirect it to a region, where it can be processed most quickly. It can also cache content and serve it from the edge, reducing network hops.

Edge networking services—including Amazon CloudFront and AWS Global Accelerator—are services that limit and consolidate requests, caching data and routing it to low-latency regions in order to deliver a great experience to customers worldwide.

A good use case is a storefront where the products don't often change, but traffic can increase and decrease dramatically when there is a sale or a particularly busy shopping season.

- **Amazon CloudFront** is a content delivery network (CDN) that enables you to run code at the edge using serverless compute. CDNs are networks of interconnected servers that speed up a web page's load time by storing data and assets geographically close to the end user. CloudFront is a cost-effective way to deliver data quickly to end users through 450+ globally dispersed points of presence (PoPs).

- A global traffic manager, **AWS Global Accelerator** allows you to connect to up to ten global regions by means of two global public IPs that act as fixed entry points to your application endpoints, which are areas closer to the end user.

CHAPTER FOUR

Camping in the Cloud

Welcome to Chapter 4. In this chapter, we dig into some of the most interesting services you can use to build your services in AWS Cloud. Specifically, we cover the following:

- Compute
- Storage
- Networking
- Databases
- Machine learning

By the end of this chapter, you will be able to differentiate between important services and understand how to use them to build your business. Let's go!

Introduction

It's time! Up to now, you've been learning about all of the interesting topics focused on preparing to build or migrate your workflows into the Cloud. But now it's time to really jump in the deep end and start considering some of the most important services that  AWS offers to help you manage your Cloud infrastructure and your data in the Cloud. This chapter discusses five big categories of services: compute, storage, networking, databases, and machine learning. Then you take a tour of the ways that you can get help setting them up and managing them.

Compute

In the context of the Cloud, the term **compute** is a general term referring to the software, hardware, resources, and objects necessary for the "computational success" of a computer program. A good explanation is here: `https://aws` `.amazon.com/what-is/compute`. In this section, we focus on some important services that help get you up and running in the AWS Cloud.

Compute Families

One of the most important services AWS offers centers on compute: EC2, which stands for Elastic Compute Cloud. The "elasticity" of this service refers to its ability to horizontally scale by adding and removing instances when needed. It's noteworthy that you can choose the "family" of compute for your EC2 instance according to your business needs.

- **General purpose:** When you need a balance of compute, memory, and network resources such as web application hosting.
- **Compute optimized:** When you have compute-intensive workloads that need high-performance processors such as scientific research that requires simulation and data analysis.
- **Memory optimized:** When you have memory-intensive workloads such as real-time processing of big data in an in-memory database system.
- **Accelerated computing:** When you have workloads needing graphics processing units (GPUs) such as training workloads for deep learning.
- **Storage optimized:** When you have workloads that need high, sequential read and write access to large datasets such as data warehousing and log processing for big data analysis and visualization purposes.

Compute Services

You already learned about EC2, but there are several other important services to help elevate your compute capacity in the Cloud. Notable are AWS Lambda, Amazon ECS, Amazon EKS, AWS Fargate, AWS Elastic Beanstalk, and AWS Outposts, discussed in Chapter 3. Let's take a look at these. It can be helpful to do a word-association exercise to match the service to its use case. Let's divide these services into two categories: serverless and fully managed.

Serverless Compute

AWS Lambda lets you run code without provisioning or managing servers. Build serverless functions in your language of choice and pay only for the compute time used by your code. Use Lambda for event-driven applications, microservices, and data processing.

Word Association: Lambda = Serverless Functions

AWS Fargate allows you to run containers without managing the underlying infrastructure. Use Fargate for containerized microservices and serverless container deployments.

Word Association: Fargate = Serverless Containers

Fully Managed Compute
Amazon Elastic Container Service (Amazon ECS) allows you to run, scale, and manage Docker containers on EC2 instances or on Fargate. Use it for containerized microservices architecture and scalable container management. Note that if ECS runs on Fargate, it's considered to be serverless.

Word Association: ECS = Docker containers

NOTE: ECS qualifies as a fully managed service.

Amazon Elastic Kubernetes Service (Amazon EKS) simplifies the deployment, management, and scaling of containerized applications using Kubernetes, a container orchestration system. Use it for managing Kubernetes workloads at scale.

Word Association: EKS = AWS's version of Kubernetes

AWS Elastic Beanstalk is a PaaS that allows you to quickly and easily deploy, manage, and scale applications. Use it for web application deployment and to reduce infrastructure complexity.

Word Association: Elastic Beanstalk = easy PaaS deployments

Auto-Scaling

One of the important aspects of working with compute in the Cloud is its inherent elasticity. Guess how that's done? By auto-scaling.

NOTE: You can also scale your capacity manually! And you can auto-scale not just compute but also storage.

Auto-scaling helps ensure that your applications can handle varying levels of traffic or workload without manual intervention. By automatically adding or removing resources based on defined policies, auto-scaling helps maintain performance, optimize costs, and improve availability.

You can control how auto-scaling is managed by setting policies, groups, triggers, and actions. Automated health checks determine when to add or remove capacity.

- **Scaling policies:** Based on CPU utilization and traffic, you define scaling policies that specify when and how your resources should be scaled.

High CPU usage? Add more capacity, and vice versa.

- **Auto-scaling groups:** Based on the scaling policies you set up, groups of resources are managed collectively to scale up or down.

- **Scaling triggers:** Set triggers to start a scaling process when a condition is met, such as a CPU increase.

- **Scaling actions:** Trigger actions such as terminating instances or adjusting the capacity of existing resources.

- **Monitoring and health checks:** Health checks automatically monitor the health of your auto-scalable instances.

Load Balancers

An elastic load balancer (ELB), as the name implies, acts as a sort of pack horse, balancing the load of incoming traffic across multiple servers or instances. They act as an intermediary between the client and the servers hosting the requested application in one or more Availability Zones. Load balancers (LBs) help your applications retain elasticity by improving their scalability.

NOTE: How does that work? ELBs balance traffic between instances so that multiple instances can serve the requests and no single instance is overloaded. Instances can be added to the target group that the ELB is sending requests to when necessary, which helps provide elasticity and scalability.

In general, ELBs provide high availability by distributing workloads. The two main ELBs are Application Load Balancer and Network Load Balancer.

- **Application Load Balancers** distribute traffic based on URLs or host headers using the HTTP and HTTPS protocols.
- **Network Load Balancers** are used for extreme scalability with low latency for large volumes of traffic, operating at the transport layer.

Storage

The previous section discussed the concept of compute and mentioned services that help you determine the type of compute you need for your business needs. This section talks about how to store assets in the Cloud. AWS has several services that enable you to store all kinds of data in the Cloud.

Amazon S3

Let's start with a classic example: Amazon Simple Storage Service (S3). When builders see S3, it's likely they think buckets! S3 buckets are containers for objects.

S3 is an object storage service where you can store all kinds of data, such as images or other files, which are stored as objects at scale. It's a service that offers 11 nines of durability.

NOTE: You learned how to define the concept of nines in Chapter 1. Note that, according to the docs, "Amazon S3 Standard, S3 Standard–IA, S3 Intelligent-Tiering, S3 One Zone-IA, S3 Glacier Instant Retrieval, S3 Glacier Flexible Retrieval, and S3 Glacier Deep Archive are all designed to provide 99.999999999% (11 9s) of data durability of objects over a given year."

S3 is a great option for managing the objects and assets you need to store while managing access, compliance, costs, and the objects' lifecycle.

Amazon S3 Glacier

Brr! Better put a coat on, with all this data archived and sitting around in cold storage! If you have data that doesn't need to be frequently accessed or a data archive that you want to store, you might use one of S3's Glacier storage classes: "Long-term, secure, durable storage classes for data archiving at the lowest cost and milliseconds access." There are three archive storage classes to choose from, depending on how you need to access your data and how long you need to store it.

- **S3 Glacier Instant Retrieval:** Access your archive data within milliseconds; an example could be a news article.

- **S3 Glacier Flexible Retrieval:** Retrieve your data within minutes or in bulk within 5 to 12 hours; an example would be a backup of data for disaster recovery.

- **S3 Glacier Deep Archive:** Fetch your data within 12 hours; an example might be archived medical data.

AWS Snowball

Need to get your data from an offline area into the Cloud? Throw a snowball! AWS Snowball helps you migrate large amounts of data into and out of the AWS Cloud using physical storage devices. After you receive your device, you connect it to your local network and write up to 80 terabytes of data to it using AWS OpsHub, NFS, or an S3 adapter. Then you ship the device back to AWS, where it's transferred to your S3 bucket, verified, and then erased from the device. The whole system is secure, trackable, and encrypted. Let it snow!

- **AWS Snowball** is part of the "snow" family, which also includes Snowmobile and Snowcone. Snowcone is a smaller device than Snowball, and Snowmobile is a big shipping container. They all serve the same purpose— moving your offline data into the Cloud.

Amazon Elastic File System

Looking for file storage in the Cloud? Amazon Elastic File System (Amazon EFS) can help you via a managed serverless Cloud file storage service that provides Network File System file storage. Create a mount point in any AWS compute service, and you'll be able to use EFS with it. Since it's elastic, it can scale to petabytes, and it can grow and shrink as you add and remove files so you don't have to manage its capacity manually.

   Amazon EFS is designed to offer low-latency access to your files across multiple Availability Zones, and it can automatically recover from hardware failures. The service removes infrequently accessed files and offers 11 nines durability and 4 nines availability.

   It can be really useful when you need to share code securely or share data across containers.

NOTE: If you need to use the specific file systems NetApp ONTAP, OpenZFS, Windows File Server, or Lustre, rather than Network File System, you can choose Amazon FSx.

Amazon Elastic Block Store

Ever wonder what an encryptable hard drive would look like in the Cloud? Amazon Elastic Block Store (Amazon EBS) is just this. You can attach block storage volumes alongside your EC2 instances to provide independent storage for your data. Since the EBS volume is independent from the instance to which it's attached, you can retain your data even if your EC2 instance is deleted.

If you have data that needs to be quickly accessible, use EBS. They can be used for file systems, databases, or other applications that need to be read and written to ad hoc, even for long-running reading and writing. In addition, you pay only for what you use.

There are two main types of EBS storage, and you should choose the one that best suits your use case.

- **Solid-State Drives (SSDs) for General Purpose and Provisioned IOPS:** These are the highest-performance volumes, and you can use them for frequently accessed, demanding transactional applications from SQL Server databases to gaming apps.

- **Hard Disk Drives (HDDs) for Throughput, Optimized, and Cold:** These are less expensive and throughput optimized for less frequently accessed workloads as well as accessing cold datasets.

AWS Storage Gateway

What if your applications are in on-premises servers, but you need them to access Cloud storage? For this use case, you need some kind of bridge between the two. AWS Storage Gateway is a good solution—it enables on-premises applications to access AWS Cloud storage. There are three types of storage gateways you can use.

- **File gateway:** This is used for file-based applications that need to transfer files back and forth from on-premises apps to the Cloud and store them in an S3 bucket or a managed file share.

- **Volume gateway:** This is used to store and manage on-premises data stored in S3 buckets. There are two modes available.

  - **Cached:** The data itself is stored in S3, and the most frequently accessed parts are stored locally in a local cache on-premises.

  - **Stored:** Most data is stored locally while also being backed up to S3.

- **Tape gateway:** Need to back up your on-premises data? Tape Gateway provides a virtual tape library for storing your backups to Amazon S3 or Amazon Glacier.

Networking

You've learned about storage and compute; now it's time to turn your attention to networking.

How can you connect the pieces of your AWS puzzle?

VPC

Wouldn't it be cool if you could have your own personal playground where you could configure all the services you like and create a custom environment just for you? Amazon Virtual Private Cloud (VPC) lets you launch all the resources you

like into a virtual network that you've configured as you like it. This virtual network can resemble any traditional network that you'd operate on your own servers, but instead it's deployed in an AWS data center.

You might need a VPC if you want to launch AWS resources, such as EC2 instances, RDS databases, and Elastic Load Balancers, in a virtual network that you need to control. An example might be a private intranet. You can use a VPC to control the experience.

Security Groups

Maybe you are concerned with controlling traffic and access to your sensitive resources and data so you need a way to ensure that only the right users are allowed administrative access to your resources. A good way to do this is to create security groups. These act as a virtual firewall, controlling inbound and outbound traffic, depending on the security rules that you set.

Each instance in a VPC, RDS instance, and LB must be associated with at least one security group. You can define inbound rules within a security group to allow specific types of traffic to reach your instances. For example, you can allow inbound traffic on port 80 to allow web traffic to reach your web server instances. By default, outbound traffic is allowed to all destinations. However, you can create specific rules to restrict outbound traffic to certain destinations or ports if you need to.

NOTE: Security groups are **stateful**, which means that outbound traffic is automatically allowed in response to valid inbound traffic.

Use security groups to manage isolation between different tiers of your infrastructure, ensuring that only the nec-essary traf-fic is allowed between components.

Amazon Route 53

You've perhaps heard of Route 66? Route 53 is something where you can also get your

kicks. Route 53 is a highly available and scalable Domain Name System (DNS). DNS, the phone-book of the Internet, translates the URL name such as `www.illustratedaws.cloud` to its mapped IP address, like 18.192.231.252. This way, when you type a URL in a browser, the DNS service can find its IP address and send you to its server to serve the content you requested. You can man-age Route 53 using the AWS CLI, using an SDK, or using  the console to configure DNS. Then you can check on the health of your lookups to make sure resources remain available.

NOTE: Route 53 is a reference to the TCP/UDP port 53, where DNS server requests are addressed.

VPN, Direct Connect

You've got your VPC all set up and configured just the way you like it. Now you need to connect your users to it, but how? You can connect it to remote networks and users using a VPN. Here are some connectivity options to consider:

- **Connecting site to site?** If you need to connect a remote site to the Cloud, use a Site-to-Site VPN to create two tunnels so that one can failover. These tunnels will connect remote devices to the Cloud.

- **Need to securely access your Cloud resources or on-premises network?** Use a Client VPN to create an endpoint for users to connect.

- **Have a bunch of sites that need to connect?** Use a VPN CloudHub to organize the communication between the network endpoints.

You can also use **AWS Direct Connect** to create a **dedicated** private connection from a remote, on-premises network to your VPC. This connection is made over an Ethernet cable, with one end connected to your router and the other to an AWS Direct Connect router. Remember, use Direct Connect if you need to bypass the public Internet, and use a VPN when it's OK to use it.

Databases

Now that you've learned about compute, storage, and networking options, you can turn your attention to the interesting topic of databases, an "electronically stored, systematic collection of data" (`https://aws.amazon.com/what-is/database`).

Amazon RDS and Aurora

Databases! There are so many different kinds, supplied by different companies with different syntax, features, and performance. In general, you can divide databases into two types: SQL and NoSQL.

NOTE: Structured Query Language (SQL) is a way to read and write data from a database by writing and running queries in that language.

Let's take a look at Amazon Relational Database Service (Amazon RDS). Not surprisingly, you can use this service to set up your relational database, a type of database that uses SQL. You use RDS to manage your favorite relational database such as MariaDB, Microsoft SQL Server, MySQL, Oracle, or PostgreSQL.

This service can help you automatically or manually back up your database and set up access. If you need to migrate your database into RDS, use the AWS Database Migration Service (DMS). If you need to convert your database engine (say, from Oracle to mySQL), use the AWS Schema Conversion Tool (AWS SCT).

If you prefer not to use a third-party relational database with RDS, you can use Amazon Aurora. Aurora is a "built for the Cloud" relational database specifically designed for MySQL and PostgreSQL databases. It's a fast option for those who already use these databases but want

to leverage the extra speed offered by Aurora as well as the ability to manage database replication and clustering, traditional pain points of these databases.

Amazon DynamoDB

You learned about relational databases, what about NoSQL databases?

NOTE: NoSQL is a type of nonrelational key-value database designed to handle and store large amounts of unstructured data. Rather than structuring data in tables as is done in a relational database, NoSQL databases store data as JSON documents.

DynamoDB is a NoSQL database service that takes care of the database management for you. Fast, reliable, and scalable, it can grow automatically to handle your data requirements. As a fully managed database, DynamoDB offers useful built-in features including security, backups, in-memory caching, automatic multiregion replication, and data import and export capabilities.

Since it can distribute your data and handle the load across multiple servers, it can offer a consistent, fast performance.

Amazon Redshift

Need a data warehouse to store massive amounts of data? Use Amazon Redshift, a fully managed data warehouse service that can store petabyte-scale data in a cost-effective way.

NOTE: A **data warehouse** is a structured system made up of tiers to store a database server, an analytics engine, and a frontend to show reports on the data. Data flows into it from various sources, including databases for analysis and reporting purposes.

If you have data lakes, other databases such as DynamoDB or streaming services, you can load data from them into your data warehouse and then query it efficiently using Redshift.

NOTE: A **data lake** is a repository that allows you to store all your structured and unstructured data at any scale. Store your data as is and analyze it using processes such as visualizations and machine learning. Your data lake might act as a feeder for your data warehouse after it's analyzed.

A serverless resource, Redshift automatically provisions and scales its workloads to access data, and you pay only for what you use when the data warehouse is in use.

Database Installation Options

You have a few choices on how you want to install your databases to handle your data requirements. You could install them on Amazon EC2, or you could instead use AWS managed databases. How can you decide?

If you choose to go the route of using EC2 to host your database, you'll need to provision your EC2 instance, connect to it, install the database

software, configure it, secure it, and handle backups and monitoring to ensure its health.

If you choose one of the many managed databases such as RDS with Aurora and DynamoDB,
your job is somewhat different. You need to go
to the console and select the type of database
you need and determine who can access it or use
IaC, the CLI, or an SDK to perform this task. Then
you let AWS or the
tools it provides
handle the scaling
and monitoring,
backing it up and
restoring it in case
of failure. AWS
handles mainte-
nance tasks as well
such as patches
and security fixes.

In general, installing your database on Amazon
EC2 gives you more control and flexibility over
the database software, but requires manual configuration and maintenance while a managed
database removes overhead and gives you a
more hands-off experience.

Machine Learning

The machines are learning! We had better pay attention and make sure they go to a good school. Machine learning refers to "the science of developing algorithms and statistical models that computer systems use to perform tasks without explicit instructions, relying on patterns and inference instead" (`https://aws.amazon.com/what-is/machine-learning`). Let's take a quick tour of the various ML services offered in the AWS Cloud.

Services for ML

Machine learning and artificial intelligence have quickly permeated our daily lives. Given training data, these systems use algorithms to spot patterns, predict trends, gain insights, and even generate new text and image content. ML can be used to predict how many tents a store will need to keep in stock, based on fluctuating weather trends using a time-series forecasting algorithm, for example. Or a generative AI system could be used to generate a personalized welcome text when you check into a campsite. The possibilities are endless.

A helpful AWS service to explore is Amazon SageMaker, which lets you build, train, and deploy ML models in the Cloud with a suite of managed infrastructure and tools.

Try running ML experiments using notebooks in the Cloud for free using SageMaker Studio Lab: `https://aws.amazon.com/sagemaker/studio-lab`.

Other ML services are specialized, including Amazon Lex, a chatbot designer; Amazon Kendra, an ML-powered enterprise search service;

Amazon Rekognition, for image and video recognition; and Amazon Textract, for text recognition.

Services for Analytics

In addition, you can leverage ML-powered analytics using an array of useful services.

- **Amazon Athena:** Analyze data "where it lives."
- **Amazon Kinesis:** Analyze streamed data such as audio, video, and IoT data.
- **AWS Glue:** Discover, prepare, and move your data from various sources into one place for analysis.
- **Amazon QuickSight:** Build business analytics dashboards.

Getting Help

Help! I need help! But where do you go to ask for help when trying to figure out the ins and outs of a given service? Fortunately, there are several types of documentation that you can consult when you really need a helping hand.

- **Following best practices:** You can't go wrong when working with the AWS Cloud if you start by being knowledgeable about best practices. In fact, following best practices is required of users, following the shared responsibility model. Have the Well-Architected Framework in mind when building; it's covered in detail in Chapter 1, and it will serve you as you work with the services. The Architecture Center will be a good resource to have at your fingertips; see `https://aws.amazon.com/architecture`.

- **Read the docs:** The AWS documentation offers authoritative information about all the services and more at `https://aws.amazon.com/documentation`.

- **re:Post:** This is a one-stop shop where you can access Knowledge Center articles and get answers from employees, community members, and partners. See `https://repost.aws`. re:Post also includes a developer forum and blogposts
- **Stack Overflow:** Developers tend to gravitate toward Stack Overflow for community answers to pressing code problems. The AWS Stack Overflow Collective is a huge community of AWS builders helping each other. See `https://stackoverflow.com/collectives/aws`.
- **Whitepapers:** The AWS docs are infused with whitepapers that dive deep into explanations about services. See `https://aws.amazon.com/whitepapers`.
- **AWS Developer Center:** Developers can visit `https://aws.amazon.com/developer` to learn more about what's new in AWS, including events and community outreach.
- **The community.aws site:** Get hands-on building tips and informative articles from community members and AWS employees at this new community hub by AWS Developer Relations.

First-Party Assistance

AWS also offers several ways for folks to find official help channels and one-on-one support. Let's take a look at your options:

- **AWS Abuse:** This is a kind of hotline; if you suspect that AWS resources are being used for nefarious activities, you can report it to the AWS Abuse Team using a Report Abuse form at

`https://support.aws.amazon.com/#/`
`contacts/report-abuse` or contact
`abuse@amazonaws.com`.

- **AWS support cases:** In the console, you can create the following three types of customer tickets to get support, depending on your support plan. All AWS customers get the Basic plan by default.

  - **Account and billing:** Customers can reach out to ask questions about billing and problems with their accounts.

  - **Service limit increase:** Customers can request a service limit increase if they are approaching limits based on their plan.

  - **Technical:** If you have more than a Basic support plan in place, you can get technical help by opening a technical case.

Premium Support

Ready to pay for support? Choose from **Developer**, **Business**, **Enterprise On-Ramp**, and **Enterprise** support plans, billed monthly. The type of support differs according to the plan you choose. Developer support and higher, for example, offer business hours web support and access to the AWS Support Slack App, but Business and higher offer 24/7 phone, web, and chat support. All the plans offer prioritized responses on re:Post. A useful table is available at `https://aws.amazon.com/premium support/plans`.

Technical Assistance

Need to ask a specific question and don't know where to start? Try **AWS IQ**, where you can ask for specific help and pay up front. It's a bit like hiring a carpenter to quickly swing by and fix a problem. You pay for these one-off tasks. AWS IQ matches you to a technical specialist to help you ASAP.

You can also contact **Professional Services**, a global team of experts, to get you and your team trained in Cloud topics. This a useful way to onboard a team via official training, some of which is free.

Finally, the **Amazon Partner Network** is a sort of "club" where you can join likeminded businesses who use the AWS Cloud. Becoming a partner can help you and your business get further training, follow curated paths to upskilling, and achieve recognition to validate your knowledge and expertise.

There are all kinds of partners, so you can find your "birds of a feather." Some are gathered around their use of various services and are called **Service Delivery Partners** or **Service Ready Partners**. Some "flock" around a business vertical like "travel and hospitality" and are called **Competency Partners**. And some are

Managed Service Providers, offering their own services on top of AWS's to solve customer needs. Some of these might be found in the **AWS Marketplace** (`https://aws.amazon.com/marketplace`), a clearinghouse of all kinds of third-party software that can help you use the AWS cloud more easily and efficiently.

CHAPTER FIVE

Being Frugal with Billing and Pricing

You've arrived at the last chapter, where we discuss the topic of billing and pricing. In this chapter, you learn about the following:

- Types of pricing, including the free tier and on-demand, reserved, and spot instance pricing
- Getting support and information about billing
- Finding information about pricing
- Alarms, alerts, and tags

By the end of this chapter, you will feel more confident about how billing works in the AWS Cloud. Let's go!

Pricing Tiers

Bills, bills, bills. What does it cost to host your workloads on AWS, and what can you expect when using these services and the bills come due? AWS bills customers based on their use of these services, with prices varying depending on the specific service and the amount you use. This section covers the various AWS payment offerings.

The Free Tier

Many AWS services offer a way to "try before you buy." Bundled as the Free Tier, there are three versions: short-term free trials, 12 months of free usage, or the "always free" options that never expire and are available to all. Check out the Free Tier avail-able in any given service to under-stand when you will start being charged, if ever, to use a service.

And be sure to watch your Billing & Cost Management dashboard to ensure that your usage matches your expectations.

Here are a few examples of the three types of Free Tier offerings:

- **12 months free:** EC2 offers 12 months of free usage, including 750 hours per month.

- **Short-term free trials:** SageMaker offers two months of free usage with limits on the number of hours available for free.

- **Always free:** DynamoDB offers 25GB of storage and up to 200 million read/write requests per month free. After that, you need to pay for what you use with costs depending on your usage model.

On-Demand Instance Pricing

You know how you have to find the shoe that fits best when hiking to avoid blisters? In the same way, you need to find the best pricing model to suit your workloads. One way to consider pricing is by subscribing to on-demand instance pricing so that you can pay as you go without any up-front commitment or long-term contract. Let's think about the best scenario for this option.

- **Variable, unplanned, infrequent, or workloads with unpredictable loads or traffic:** If your application experiences periodic spikes in usage or unpredictable up-and-down traffic levels, you can use on-demand pricing.

- **Just trying it:** If you just want to run a quick test of a workload, you could provision it quickly, pay for it as you run the test, and then delete it. For this purpose, you could try on-demand pricing. This scenario can also work when you want to try different sizes of instances to find your application's best fit.

- **One-time tasks:** If you're running a one-off batch process, a quick data analysis, or any one-time task, on-demand pricing might work well for you.

On-demand pricing is great for unpredictable, flexible workloads requiring no commitment, but it can be more expensive. When your requirements settle down, you might choose a different pricing model, like reserved or spot instances, both of which are discussed in the following sections.

Reserved Instance Pricing

What if your traffic doesn't experience unexpected spikes, or you have identified usage patterns that make logical sense? In this case, you might graduate to *reserved instances*, also known as RIs. RIs offer a way to lock in a rate for your most predictable workloads. This pricing option can offer cost savings over on-demand pricing, so let's examine the kind of workloads you can run on an RI.

- **Steady, mission-critical, long-term workloads:** If you can predict the workload's usage, you can optimize your costs. By committing to a specific instance type and term, you can lock in a lower hourly rate than on-demand. Use RIs for workloads that must have high availability and good performance.

- **Mix and match:** If your workload is mostly consistent but has some spikes that are harder to predict, you can use an RI for the baseline and then add on-demand or spot instances to handle peak loads.

Flexibility

Although it might seem as if you need to strictly define your RIs before deploying them, they actually are built with some flexibility to accommodate changes, depending on the plan you choose. Let's take a look:

- **Instance size flexibility:** Swap your RIs with other instances in the same family, as described in Chapter 4, as long as that instance has the same or lower compute units.

- **Availability Zone flexibility:** Deploy your RI into any Availability Zone in the same region when needed.

- **Modifications and exchanges:** Modify or convert your RIs to adapt to your needs, such as changing their instance size or network platform. You can also exchange them for another instance type in the same family.

RIs in AWS Organizations

If you've organized your accounts into an AWS Organization, RIs have some interesting benefits. An *AWS Organization* is an account management service that allows you to group and centrally manage accounts. You can consolidate and manage payments across all the linked accounts. You can allow all the linked accounts to use the Ris, and you can consolidate the RI billing to enable cost sharing and centralized account and billing management. This is helpful since you have paid up front for RIs and now can use them across your various accounts, as needed.

Spot Instance Pricing

Ever wonder what happens to compute capacity that goes unused? Does it somehow disappear? What a waste that would be! Instead, you have the ability to place a bid to grab some unused capacity for your quick-running, one-off compute needs when it becomes available. You're bidding on what are called *spot instances*. Like an auction, their price depends on demand. Use them when you need a lot of flexibility rather than a guarantee of long-term availability.

WARNING: Watch out! When spot instances pricing outpaces your bid, your service can be interrupted. Consider depending on a hybrid array of on-demand, RIs, and spot instances to ensure good availability.

Spot instances are useful for the following:

- **Batch processing and data analysis** such as video transcoding, scientific simulations, and other tasks that can be divided into independent one-off chunks. A good example is a financial analysis task, such as risk modeling that runs on occasion.

- **Testing, development systems, and CI/CD pipelines** that don't need 100 percent uptime but run occasionally.

- **Data mining and machine learning**, which are computationally intensive but don't run constantly. Good examples are training a model, running a deep learning algorithm, and tuning hyper-parameters.

- **Stateless and fault-tolerant apps** that don't require high uptime.

Getting Billing Support and Information

Lost? Confused? Surprised by a bill? You may need some support. In this section, you learn about the various places you can find information and support on billing.

Cost Explorer, Billing Conductor, and AWS Budgets

Billing is a challenging area of expertise. It's one thing to look at a spreadsheet of your costs and an entirely different thing to visualize it with the view of cost optimization. You can use some of the AWS tools to break down your AWS spending so you can better understand where your money is going and where you can find potential savings.

NOTE: You can control access to details about billing by using IAM roles.

- **AWS Cost Explorer:** AWS Cost Explorer is all about billing insights. Where are you spending the most? Where could you find savings? Cost Explorer helps you visualize and analyze your AWS costs and usage via charts, graphs, and reports that show your spending over time. It also helps you forecast your future costs and helps you discover spending patterns and anticipate and prevent any billing surprises.

- **Billing Conductor:** Billing Conductor, just like a train's conductor, lets you gather multiple accounts into one group so you can manage their billing via parameters and generate reports for the entire group. It's most useful for AWS Solution Providers and Enterprise customers.

- **AWS Budgets:** AWS Budgets offers preemptive help in setting budgets and alerting you to when they are reaching their thresholds. A proactive monitor, AWS Budgets helps you stay within your budget limits, whether for specific accounts, linked accounts, or tagged account groups.

Think of AWS Cost Explorer as a tool for in-depth visualization and analysis

EXPLORER

CONDUCTOR

BUDGET

of your AWS costs and usage data. Billing Conductor groups accounts into one neat, billable entity. AWS Budgets is a proactive tool to help you avoid unexpected billing spikes.

Consolidated Billing

You've already read about AWS Organizations, which provide a way for you to consolidate various accounts to streamline your processes. AWS Organizations include a management account that manages member accounts. This comes in handy as you grow your business and add accounts. Consolidated Billing is a free, helpful tool to streamline your bills. You get the following:

- Just one bill for all your accounts
- A good way to track charges across all the accounts
- A way to combine the usage across your multiple accounts and thereby benefit from volume discounts

By using Consolidated Billing to group your accounts' details, you can save time and money.

AWS Cost and Usage Report and Market-place Tools

So far, you've read about the "roll-up" type tools that give you insights into usage trends and spending that your account or accounts are incurring. What if you want to do a deep dive into your costs? In this case, you'd want to take a look at the CUR—the Cost and Usage Report. AWS CUR is exported as a multipage report with flexible columns so you can customize it to your needs.

Use AWS CUR to dig into individual costs in depth and analyze them in detail. It can help you dig into how your RIs are incurring costs and find on-demand pricing availability. This report will help you decide when to move eligible work-loads into a more appropriate pricing model. You can format the report to refresh the billing charges and fine-tune your spending by getting granular data. You can also upload these reports into Amazon QuickSight or Amazon Redshift to analyze your costs in a format that's famil-iar to you.

Looking for more help managing your costs, usage, and billing issues? Stop by the AWS Mar-ketplace for third-party tools that might help you analyze your costs, discover potential optimiza-tions to implement, automate your billing pro-cesses, and set up monitoring and alerts to help manage your billing thresholds.

Billing Support and the Enterprise

Despite your best effort to stop cost overruns and manage your usage, you might still need to get help from AWS Support. Don't panic! All customers, regardless of their support level, can ask for help via the AWS Management console in the Account and Billing Support Case area. Go to AWS Support and open a ticket if you have any questions about your billing.

The highest level of support available is Enterprise Support. You receive "white-glove" support to help you optimize your AWS environment and achieve your business objectives. Specifically to help with billing, you are provided with billing experts who specialize in working with accounts and can help you with any billing questions.

Finding Pricing Information on AWS Services

You've learned about billing and know how to find support, so now it's time to learn about pricing.

AWS Pricing Calculator and the Price List API

Everyone wants to know how much a given service will cost! Want to take a look at your potential pricing without building out your infrastructure, or curious about how changing your setup on AWS might impact your bottom line? Try the free AWS Pricing Calculator, a web app that helps you estimate the costs of your use cases. Use it to make better decisions on how you want to allocate your spending to best suit your needs and goals.

The Calculator is located at `https://calculator.aws`, and it's quite handy to see the costs associated with your chosen services and their configurations. That way, you can better estimate the costs of your infrastructure. You can sort these estimates into groups, share them via a link, and export them to CSV or PDF files.

The data behind the Pricing Calculator comes from the AWS Price List API. You can query this API for a list of current prices or historical pricing data related to a service. Use this data directly to display pricing data in places other than the Calculator. It can return pricing data as a JSON object or a CSV file, so you can embed this data in your applications, as needed.

Product Pages Pricing

Another excellent way to discover the pricing associated with the services you need is to visit their given product pages at `https://aws.amazon.com`. Use the drop-down menu at the top to discover how each product and service is priced via their individual pricing pages in the secondary menu. You can also visit the Pricing page at `https://aws.amazon.com/pricing` to filter products and services by pricing type.

Alarms! Alerts! Tags!

When bills start to accrue, it's best to be notified proactively. In this section, you learn about alarms, alerts, and tags. In this context, an **alarm** is a process you can configure to fire when a certain condition is met, such as when a billing threshold is exceeded. Before setting up an alarm, enable billing **alerts**, which monitor your billing charges. **Tags** are labels that can be assigned to a resource to help track your costs— AWS uses these tags to categorize your costs so they are clearly marked on your billing reports.

Alarms and Alerts

One of the smartest things you can do when setting up applications in the Cloud is to set an alert to notify you when your bill exceeds a threshold you set. Enable these alarms by visiting your account's Billing console to set up monitoring for your services. You need to add the email address to notify once a given cost threshold has been exceeded. Behind the scenes, these alerts use Amazon CloudWatch to monitor for the charge and Amazon SNS to send the email. Since you can use up to 10 alarms and 1,000 email notifications free each month as part of the AWS Free Tier, go ahead and set them up!

Tagging for Cost Allocation

Another savvy way to track your costs and avoid surprises is to use cost allocation tags, supported by many services. AWS can generate cost allocation tags automatically, but if you want finer control over how tags are used to identify cost-incurring services, create user-defined cost allocation tags. Activate tags in the Billing console to match the environment that you have set up in a given service. Tag, you're it!

Conclusion

Throughout the journey on which you embarked in this illustrated guide to the AWS Cloud, you dove into interesting and important topics that introduced some of the major aspects of becoming a builder in the AWS Cloud. You started by packing the camper as you embarked on an introduction of Cloud computing concepts, including learning about the benefits of the Cloud, AWS Cloud economics, the concept of the "total cost of ownership," reducing costs by moving to the Cloud, Cloud architecture design principles, and finally that useful model that helps you build

efficiently in the Cloud: the Well-Architected Framework.

Then, you made sure that once en route, you had packed those bear-proof containers and bug spray by getting a solid foundation of security and compliance in the Cloud. You learned specifics around the shared responsibility model, access management, including use of IAM, and resources to support you in your quest to stay safe in the Cloud.

Next, you pitched your tent in Camp AWS, learning about the various ways you can deploy resources and workloads in the Cloud, including how and where to connect and build infrastructure. You learned about Availability Zones, Regions, and Edge Locations. You also learned about specific services you can use in the AWS Cloud, focusing on compute, storage, networking, databases, machine learning, and where to get help configuring them. Finally, you were introduced to all the ways you might have to pay the bills and how pricing works.

We hope that you enjoyed this foray into the vast camping ground that is AWS and that you used the images to help you remember the concepts. It's your book, so feel free to color the images as a relaxation technique if you're preparing for the Cloud Practitioner Certification exam. Finally, visit the accompanying website at `https://awsillustrated.cloud` for supplemental materials, including reference links and learning opportunities to help deepen your understanding.

Happy camping from Jen and Denise!